Cuarentena

Cuarentena

A Collection of Forty Poems

Steve Lang

RESOURCE *Publications* · Eugene, Oregon

Resource Publications
An Imprint of Wipf and Stock Publishers
199 W. 8th Ave., Suite 3
Eugene, OR 97401

www.wipfandstock.com

PAPERBACK ISBN: 978-1-6667-1658-0
HARDCOVER ISBN: 978-1-6667-1659-7
EBOOK ISBN: 978-1-6667-1660-3

JUNE 28, 2021

For Jacqui

Contents

Acknowledgements

The author is grateful to the editors of the following magazines who first published poems in the collection as follows:

Ariel Chart International Literary Journal—*Raphael, The Watchman, Exile, Hamaca, The Ark*
Grand Little Things—*Hymn to Ninkasi, I'll get on my knees, The Maimed, The Foolish Man, Lourdes*
Plum Tree Tavern—*The Fig and the Wasp*
Indian Periodical—*Love Poem, Push-back*
Oddball Magazine—*Fallen*
Unearthed Literary Magazine—*Relict, Orchid*
BeznCo—*Humility*
Chiron Review—*After the Bowstring Broke*
The Galway Review—*Columbina, Tilma*

Preface

We have the word "quarantine" from the Venetian word *quarentena*, meaning "forty days," being the number of days a ship entering the port of Venice must spend in isolation in the days of The Black Death.

Very few of the poems in this collection are directly about the Covid-19 pandemic but all are somehow of it. They were written over a twelve-month period beginning March 2020 in El Salvador, hence the Spanish title, and there are 40 of them.

i

Raphael

From all the thrones and dominions,
The powers and principalities,
One must come, a nation-guardian;
A healer to stir the cool waters
In Bethesda, House of Mercy,
From which the paralyzed man emerged
Renewed, through the central portico,
Blinking at the bright, ascending sun,
One contentious Sabbath morning.
Teach us, messenger, the prayer of Cordoba,
For the crown prince of demons,
Your old foe, is unbound–
Claw-footed, water-hater,
Lame devil, crowned cambion,
Slayer of our bride's seven unfulfilled suitors–
While we wait forlorn at our wedding feast,
Our graves pre-dug on the edge of town,
Our father's inheritance
Unclaimed.

ii

The Fig and the Wasp

Desperate, she burrows into soft flesh,
Shedding her subtle, ethereal wings
That sped her on this single flight,
The clandestine bloom obliging,
Towards the pulpy pouch, wherein,
She'll disgorge her treasured eggs and die.
Her brood will mate and fly the fig,
The females on their final flight,
Pregnant and, unknowing, tagged
With sticky, figgy sex-dust,
To proliferate perpetual fruit
That feeds the needful forest from
The generous parasite, keystone strangler,
Hollow-latticed, steep cathedral,
From which Hathor herself evolves,
To welcome home each weary soul.

iii

Rainbow

Reach ruby, for the engorged throat,
Gaping gallus[1] at your genial threat.
Graze the galaxy of his travelled arms;
Diminish them of their burnished bronze.
Scrape the crusted, jaundiced debris
From the lashes of his sallow eyes,
Once lit like bright-bedeckled fern,
Quick pictish wit and glowing erin,
Now haunted, half-life, hinterlands,
Stirred only by your midnight fiends,
Woad-wolves shadowing a shambling shell,
Purpling the forest floor at will,
Finally bursting the flaccid sack
That fades from violet to ivory and black.

1. Scots slang- Blithely overconfident, swaggering

After the Bowstring Broke

Not today,
With Magdalene at the empty tomb,
Having shuffled the mighty stone aside
Diligently, night by numbing night;
Head-bowed, eyes closed, prays the pilgrim,
Reaching for his pain again
With intuitive, devoted fingers,
Vessel to the wind that sang
Through him, with him and in him,
That filled the arc of his aching sails
And carried us over the Jordan.

But back here, stuck, at the junction,
Hunched below the broken clock,
His beanie pulled down low,
His Gibson planted neck-deep,
Beside him in red Delta dirt,
Like a country bus-stop marker,
Or macabre, hollow headstone
For the grave of the very same devil,
Who might be here,
Tomorrow.

Found wanting

You want wisdom?
I think I understand,
But have you tried
Your brother,
The quiet
One?

You want kindness?
Did you consider
The fluttering tramp,
You only gave
A wide berth to?

You blame me?
I sense your
Silent
censure

You want forgiveness?
To be clear,
In truth,
Exoneration.

You want courage?
I fear
You too,
Must find your own.

You want love?
Here it is;
It was here all along.

You want perfection?
My dear,
My own,
My poor child.

The Maimed

I sat at his feet that day,
On the mountain,
When he wiped away my tears,
And the vast throng
Shielded their eyes in wonder
At the miracle of
My new-found integrity;
But, while the fish and the bread were doled out,
I wondered how long
I could make it last.

vii

I'll get on my knees[1]

"I can't breathe"
They did not understand him
"I need some water"
Why is my language not clear to you?
"Everything hurts"
The invalid replied
"I'm sorry; I'm so sorry!"

"They're gonna kill me, man"
I have no-one to help me
"Mama, Mama, Mama!"
Stop sinning or something worse may happen

"Let him breathe!"
The law forbids you
"Don't kill me!"
You judge by human standards
"I'm about to die"
No one ever spoke like this man!

1. Audio recording of the arrest of George Floyd May 25th 2020, alternating with quotations from John 7 and 8

Humility

I threw my father's gold-filled pouch,
Proud in rage, upon the dust,
By the sandals of the stubborn priest,
Whose shabby, crumbling, Umbrian church,

In praise of the sainted, silverless twin,
Physician to the Syrian poor,
I would, in time, and sweat, repair
By hand, stone by beggared stone;

But first, emerging, on bare feet,
I cross the bones around my cave,
Tenderly, thus, escape my grave,
Past dainties foes would have me eat,

To disdain my tainted clothes for justice,
Stand naked before God and man,
Bereft of every vestment, chain,
Let and hindrance to true service;

Then, to the Mount of the god of thieves,
To meditate, to find the words
For a sermon to my brethren birds
And courage to covenant with wolves.

Through the Sultan's fire I pass
Unscathed, to witness to Your truth,
I kiss the leper on his mouth
And scold the sovereign for excess.

I never shrank from Your command
But now must slip my false foes' snare,
Escape alone, as David's prayer
Slips from my bleeding hand.[1]

1. October 3rd, 2020- 796 years to the day since the death of St Francis of Assisi

ix

Tilma

Do not fear sickness,
For at the hidden river,
I'll appear once more
To the dutiful nephew,
Array his red flowers
That tumble headlong
From his humble mantle,
To reveal, not me,
But my vivid impression;
Then recall my words
To him and you
And that poor soul
With the arrow in his neck:
Am I not here,
I, who am your mother,
Your shadow and protection,
Your fountain of joy,
Commissioned by One
Whose hologram yet haunts
All three chambers
Of my inner eye?[1]

1. 12/12/2020 Dia de la Virgen de Guadalupe

x

Columbina

This queenly, cinnamon Columbina,
With a flourish, instantly self-defined,
Flowers reverently fading behind her,
Serenely swinging on her orchid vine,

Watching me unperturbed, poised and calm,
Perhaps the same I nursed, soft-cooing,
Cradled in close-cupped, prayerful palms,
Stroking and searching her silken wing,

Feeling with dread for the jagged break,
Yet here now, self-composed and whole,
A scraggle of straw in her sweet-peck beak
For the nest she's building over the wall,

In some fruitful, fragrant, tamarind tree,
Elsewhere, apart from this arbor and me.

xi

Arena

Impervious abrasive
Ultimate diminution
Erosion's expert and emolument just
Witnessed by stars
Decrypted by time
Binding our bricks cohering
Our concrete fixing our mortar setting
Our stage
Grains as groundstars unspaced
Unlit metaphor for myriad
Shifts like a simile
Broken beyond breaking
Worn to a worry
A hone a grind
A sharpener for our blade
A measure for our measure

xii

Dylan's Worm

Mouthing forward lightless, eyeless,
Ganglian-guided, colorless kill,
Susceptible and skinny phallus,
Plying sea, sand, silt and loam,
Clay, bright-wet-pink,
Or black-ripe flesh,
Compartmentalised,
Egregious, solitary grazer,
Relentless, indiscriminate
Reformer and regenerator,
Ploughing his own womb,
Not sexless, but self-sexing,
Humble scion of Salcamis.

xiii

Orchid

Little angel
With your diamond crown
Bridal veil
Pink slippers lurid
Adder's mouth
Resupine
All wanton inflorescence
Labellum swollen fused
In vanilla inner whorl
I will melt you will cry
And down among the coral-roots
Between the leopards and the swans
The mirrors scorpions jewels and ghosts
Our column conjoins our clade

Lady's Slipper

Hanging by a whip-thin, fragile tendril,
Seam between realms imagined, endured,
A single maroon-butter, pendant vagina,
Delicate sculptured, voluptuous conchita;
Blow sweetly there, behold space shudder,
Time tremble to the tiny, golden trumpet;
Succumb to a kiss of cool, dew-water nectar
From this gilded slipper, soft, radiant spark,
The universe wheels reverently round.

Push-back

Staring, black-blinded, past distance,
I am startled by a sudden, sub-atomic flare:
A tremendous, shocking, silent tremor,
That left and reached, at once,
Everywhere,
In water, leaf and rock,
Push-back:
Seismic wave in space and air
And time to come, and past,
Distinct, but only just discernible,
Tremble of an eyeball to a pulse,
Or flutter of meniscus,
In a font,
Before the blast.

xvi

Ser/Estar

Slung between two muscular
Branches of Andromeda,
In a womb of space,
A worm of time,
I sense, so strong,
My ancience,
How fully, now, I
Occupy
This untrammeled moment,
Immortal in this instant,
Suspended perfect as,
That pregnant orange sunset
Or these luscious red tomatoes,
Ripening implacably.

xvii

Hamaca

From the length of rope, flung
Over the rough, black truss
And tied in the slip-knot,
I tighten myself,
Limply swinging,
Head to one side,
Finally absolved,
Excused, cocooned;
Reimagined as Joseph,
Promoted vizier,
Touring heaving grain barns,
Suspended in my canvas chariot,
In the distance, a dreadful chitter
Of untold locust wings.

xviii

Oblation

Borne
Toward
Swelling
Fertile
Suffered
Carried
Away
Ablation
Absence
Being
Away
Hence
Being
Still.

xix

Littoral

A winter's evening,
On the glistening, wide,
Amaranthine shore,
Above me arched a bruising sky,
And dimmed a little,
At my feet,
Myself,
With the sun
Setting over my shoulder,
Arms flung wide,
Parsing my life,
Like my own horizon,
Or sentry holding back
The thronging tide
Of conscience,
The surge and crash
And running out
Of memory;
The wet sand still betrays
No signs yet
Of the footprints
Of the one who rushes to enfold me
In one last and lasting,
Rapturous embrace

Ebb-tide

At ebb-tide, on a winter's evening,
When the wind and cold are breathtaking,
And the clear, damp light
Washed-out, insipid,
There, in the time-scraped,
Humorless mud-sand
A furious scuffle of footprints,
Toe-to-toe;
The torque and twist of the tussle
Betrayed by banked-up ramparts,
Deep-carved heel-holes,
Arcing trenches, and kicked-up sand-spray
The glistening, grainy, saline silt
Patiently assimilates,
So that, in time, no sign remains
Of the middle-aged, duffled-up waltzers,
Who inscribed on the staveless shore-flats,
Their tender eventide love-song
In turns, returns,
Quick skips, and skirls,
Rises, falls, and timeless holds,
As spirited, and as carefree as,
The dancing bobbles
On their woolly hats.

xxi

Late Afternoon Sunlight

Late afternoon sunlight

On a cloudless day
In El Salvador

So pure
And placid
And appalling

Exile

This day, seven and more centuries ago,
Not fourscore years since the Magna Carta,
Longshanks issued his "Edict of Expulsion",
To exile, once more, the Israelites,
Degraded by infantile blood libel
And yellow badges of two tablets joined,
Symbolising the sacred stones,
Blood covenant, hallowed in a gilded box,
Tabernacled during the desert exodus
But lost, just as its successor,
Articulated on the mount,
Anticipated in the upstairs room,
Authorised at Golgotha:
See, now, *Missouri Man* barefoot,
Astride his treasured, tainted temple,
His wintry palace built on broken bones,
Assault rifle cradled across his paunch,
Disgorging the displaced, untrespassing
Multitudes from his specious eden,
Through the gates they entered by,
Still standing there, unbroken.

xxiii

The Ruined Slope

Echoes the cry, earth's mighty heave,
Blank rocks cleave; the arras is rent,
The suicide's bloody silver spent,
On my bleached bones in an exile's grave,
A wanderer's last dusty stop,
In the potter's field,
My tomb still sealed,
At the foot of the ruined slope.

Limbo

I've hung around riverbanks before
Waiting for dutiful ferries at night
But in this hush the float and flight
Of feathery wisps along the shore

Embers wheeling shaping shifting
Shiny fine black sooty slivers
Blaze-blown whimsical scintillas
Insensible to touch and drifting

So thick that all is a grainy grey
Failings fall in shudders of regret
Ashes fasten to my bloodied feet
Layering the lashes of my resigned eye

xxv

The Uncommitted

In half-light, the haunted,
Gaunt, glaikit haints howl,
Grey murmuration of the vain and vacant,
Swarming after the bright flag's furl,
Cyphers deserving no blame or praise,
With their slack-jawed mouths and unlit eyes.

Towering totems loom, dread ring
Of blank obsidian, mirroring marble,
Imprisoning wraiths, the shining double
Of those that screech at each hornet's sting,
While tears and blood and pus and sweat
Feed grateful maggots around their feet.

Tantalised, they skirl and whirl
And wail behind the banderole,
With wasps and worms for company,
Unworthy of hell's infamy,
While pearl, on fire, above them shone,
On the ash-strewn shores of Acheron.

xxvi

Hymn to Ninkasi

Schooled gently by the attentive
Temple harlot, I paid good heed
To the advice for Gilgamesh
So, satisfied by my portion, withdraw,
Relinquish my vain and arrogant quest,
Descend twin peaks, down the road of the sun,
Passing, once more, the scorpion lovers,
And the serpent's dry, discarded skin,
To arrive astonished, on the golden shore;
White the waves rise, white the waves fall,
Onrush of coolness overcomes,
And I awake, like Hathor,
To music, laughter, sky,
And gratitude.

xxvii

Serpent

Trail the scud-sleek, sinuous,
Vital cord of cold chub-muscle,
Bullet-head zip-lipped, imperious-
Impervious, implacable,

Thithering through the warm-tilled earth
Of ghosts, regrets and gallusness,
Haunts of earnest, blighted youth
Or creeping lithe and limbless,

Shifting cool, whispering ashes in the urn,
So feathery light the grey memories,
That stick, as dust, to the black-forked tongue
And the teardrop, slick and viscous.

xxviii

The Kiss

Lips sting sweet at the smoky kiss,
Instant blessing, time-proof tarnish;
The self-delusion of glib collusion
With hags as filthy as the one
Lugubrious, in this hell of mirrors,
Betraying back my nobler Banquos,
Blank widening eye of the speculum,
To the crack of self-inflicted doom.

Drowning Out

How I wish I could stop me,
Haul up the needle,
Swing through the mute air,
Cradle me down;

But I bow to my charmer,
Blunting my diamond,
Riding your cryptic
Groove round and round,

While I channel your lightning,
My black spiral tightening;
Slide to the center,
And silently drown.

Hands Down

I curled round your finger,
Fuddled your black hair,
Lit you like a Chinese
Lantern, I guess.

And I still bear the scar of
The nail you pushed in me,
Penance, I suppose,
For your fecklessness.

Now I stroke the grey chin of
The ghost in the corner;
Tap out the dregs,
Like I could care less.

The Necklace

You've never fully fathomed
The depths of our depravity,
Till you've seen the baying crowd pursue
A thief with dreadful confidence,
One prescient loping hollow youth,
Wide, ancient dead-eyes fixed ahead,
Toting the ready tire.

xxxii

La Esperanza

El Avioncito

Here, the little plane
Dangles from the ceiling,
So slowly swinging overhead,
Hanging heavy,
Prayerless botafumeiro
In this unholy place;
Hear the creak of rope,
The rafters' groan,
And, fainter still,
The whimper,
Of a broken man
Still breaking

La Capucha

Here, in our future museum,
This theatre of the past,
Still hopeless, the pitiful damned,
And their pitiless, damned tormentors,
Perform their danse macabre:
Enter stage right La Capucha
With his shiny-black, eyeless
Football for a head,

Upstage, the bone-white, brim-full bath,
Stage centre, the squat car battery,
Concentrating heaviness,
Sprouting from either terminal,
Two hypnotic scream-squiggles
Of stripped-back wire;
And, as our flushed guide,
Ingratiates, a-hem, for attention,
I wonder how thoroughly,
And how many times,
They scrubbed these walls
Of their crusted blood,
Before painting them
An inoffensive grey.

La Hamaca

Here, at the enchanted place,
In painstakingly chosen,
Designer swim-shorts,
See them heave, in rhythm,
The lithe, laughing muchacho,
By his feet and hands,
Arcing into clean air
And refreshing water;
Now see them again
In grimy drab uniform,
Under a bare bulb's
Unblinking stare,
Swing him as hard
Into the bloodstained wall
Then bend down wearily,
As campesinos to a deadweight
Sack of plush coffee beans,
To do so.....once again.....here.

xxxiii

La Viuda

The oblique, old widow made her reprise,
Singing her whispered parting song,
At the sullen meat-packing plant,
In dissolute Santa Ana,
Five heinous days
In August,
1981.

Excruciating hush of her well-honed caesura,
    Before the clunk of wide-eyed heads,
        Eighty-three of them, all told,
            In the blood-stained pail.

xxxiv

Relict

The slick-black-glassy basalt
Betrays a flipper's hesitance,
Recoiling at gravity's swift assault,
His blubber shudders on the precipice,
And in the pregnant, pendant
Moment, bulbous panicked eyes
Never were so prescient,
As, scrabbling tragically, he slides
Into breathless air, to land
With unechoed thud, an instant husk,
Lifeless on the rocky, oil-black strand,
With his jagged stump of shattered tusk
A broken vein to a simpler time:
A world where walruses need not climb.

The Watchman

The watchman I set long ago
Declares now for you what I saw
And foresaw: dire vision–
A whirlwind from the barren places,
The spoiler despoils, trades in treachery,
While the avaricious feast on flesh,
Quaff from mildew-tainted vessels
Looted from the silent ruins
Of the covenant's holy sanctuary.
See my spectral hand scratch out
Our epitaph upon our wall,
The number of our days,
The damning verdict of the scales,
The names of our noble nemeses;
We may oil our shields and whet our swords
Or vainly flee from the taut-flexed bow
Under the arc, within the compass
Of the intuitive, unerring bolt,
The final, fatal missive,
Forthwith profoundly fathomed,
Felling us forward to oblivion;
Meanwhile, the good-holder, winged young sun,
This very hour, bestows with care
Humiliation on the bloated lion.

xxxvi

Fallen

False accuser, slanderer,
Sly, mendacious mind-infector,
With honey for your backbiters,
And ashes for the lips of orphans;
Plague inflictor, desert tempter,
Chief of lascivious, cave-dwelling Watchers,
Languish now in the poisoned well,
Where perfidious, recreant traitors lie
Ice-bound in the ninth dominion,
Condemned forever, frozen fast,
Gallant Michael's laceration
Festering fetid in your side,
One of your three bloated faces
Gnawing on the bones of Judas.

El Zonte

Swell and furl and looming breast,
Crash stinging, strict as salt, and harsh,
Resound on gnarled-black-blasted rocks,
Shuddering the sand-shelved shore,
This moon-bathed bluff,
Where pulses faint
My febrile heart,
My soul unbound,
In foundless and unfathomed,
Black, swirling whorl of succubi,
Incubi, as I, their cambion, descend,
My arms akimbo, head bowed limp,
The viscous, unforgiving void,
A flailing wraith my zenith.

xxxviii

Lourdes

In Lourdes,
A dead man is borne on a stretcher,
Not by his family,
But to them.

But he was not their patriarch
So the eldest son was sent for him,
To search below in anguish,
Among the indiscriminate corpses.

xxxix

Cuarenta

The length of a fast or an inundation,
The price in acres of a pioneer;
The age to hear Gabriel's revelation,
The paragraphs in a Sikh's daily prayer.
The cycle of a Hebrew generation,
The full term of a pregnancy;
The objects of a Buddhist meditation,
The Venetian *quaranta giorni.*

The lashes of a Sanhedrin sentence,
Minus one, for avoidance of error,
So, emerging from quarantine penance,
We stumble forward in terror,
Of the last stroke, held in abeyance

xl

YHWH

He who will be
And who is
Being endlessly
Beginning

In the word
With the word
Of the word
The word

Printed in Great Britain
by Amazon

71903712R00037